# B.C.
# STAR LIGHT, STAR BRIGHT, FIRST...

by Johnny Hart

FAWCETT GOLD MEDAL • NEW YORK

Published by Fawcett Gold Medal Books, a unit of CBS Publications, the
Educational and Professional Publishing Division of CBS, Inc.

ISBN 0-449-12365-0

Printed in the United States of America

First Fawcett Gold Medal Edition: December 1982

10   9   8   7   6   5   4   3   2   1

6-8

6-9

6·22

6·23

UN-BEAK THAT WORM, OR I'LL COME OUT THERE AND TIE YOUR FACE IN A KNOT!

6-25

THE END JUSTIFIES THE MEANNESS.

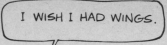

6·26

6.29

7·1

7-2

7.3

7.5

7-6

7-8

7-9

7-12

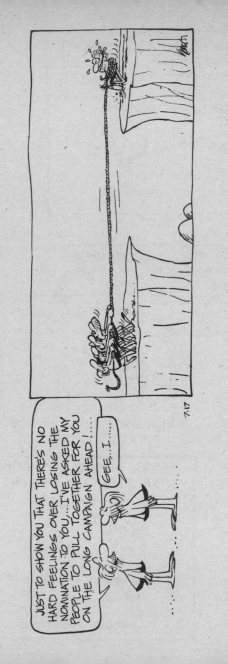

7-22

7·24

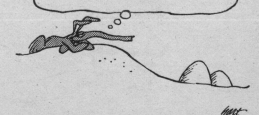

BANG

7·27

7.30

7·31

8-2

8.4

8-9

8-10

8·23

8-28

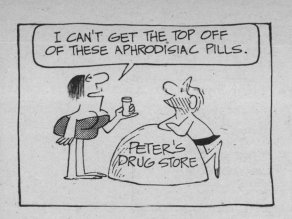

9.2

9.3

9-6

9·18

♡ YOU MAY NOT KNOW IT, WILEY, BUT WE HAVE A LOT IN COMMON ♡

9-27

IN WHAT WAY?

WE HAVE THREE FEET BETWEEN US.

9:30

genius: *n*

10·1

a mistaken attribute usually applied to a master of vagueness.

10.4

10-5

10·6

197

10.8

10.9

10-11

10.13

HEY, LISTEN TO THIS HOT ITEM IN THIS MORNING'S PAPER,...

10·14

I READ EVERY SINGLE WORD IN THAT CRUMMY RAG, FROM THE BANNER ON THE FRONT PAGE TO THE LAST PERIOD ON THE BACK PAGE INCLUDING THE DATES AND PAGE NUMBERS.

...HOW LONG HAVE YOU BEEN HARBORING THIS PARTICULAR PEEVE, SWEETUMS...?

10-19

DO YOU BELIEVE MAN'S DESTINY IS CONTROLLED BY THE STARS?

YOU'RE DARN RIGHT! ...LET'S FACE IT,.....

10·20

WE DRINK JOE DIMAGGIO'S COFFEE, WEAR JOHNNY CARSON'S SUITS, RIDE IN BOB HOPE'S CARS AND EAT ANN BLYTH'S TWINKIES.

11.3

11-22

11-26

STRUT    STRUT

11-27

EUREKA!... I'VE INVENTED THE FREEZER!

STRUT
STRUT
STRUT
STRUT
STRUT
STRUT
STRUT
STRUT

11-29

12·1